Hopscotch
GIRLS

I am confident, Brave & Beautiful

A Coloring Book for Girls

This book is all about building a girl's confidence,
imagination, and spirit. We hope these coloring pages
will encourage girls to think beyond social conventions
and inspire conversations with the adults in their lives
about what it really means to be
confident, brave, and beautiful.

◦ ❥ ♡ ◦◦ ❥ ♡ ◦◦ ❥ ♡ ◦◦ ◦ ❥ ♡ ◦◦ ❥ ♡ ◦

Dedicated to Errie Rose
and every other little bud that is
about to bloom into something wonderful.

I am Brave

I am Curious

I am Beautiful

I am Powerful

I am Sincere

I am Clever

I am Analytical

I am Capable

I am
Brave, Curious,
Inventive, Beautiful,
Bright, Kind, Powerful,
Creative, Intelligent,
Sincere, Strong, Clever,
Loving, Analytical,
Independent, Confident,
Tenacious, Capable

I am
all of this
and
so much more

I AM ME!